HOW TO LOSE WEIGHT
ON A FLEXITARIAN DIET

A Delicious and
Nutritious Way to
Reach Your
Ideal Weight

Jerry Carr

LEGAL & DISCLAIMER

The information contained in this book and its contents is not designed to replace or take the place of any form of medical or professional advice; and is not meant to replace the need for independent medical, financial, legal, or other professional advice or services, as may be required. The content and information in this book has been provided for educational and entertainment purposes only.

The content and information contained in this book has been compiled from sources deemed reliable, and it is accurate to the best of the Author's knowledge, information, and belief. However, the Author cannot guarantee its accuracy and validity and cannot be held liable for any errors and/or omissions. Further, changes are periodically made to this book as and when needed. Where appropriate and/or necessary, you must consult a professional (including but not limited to your doctor, attorney, financial advisor, or such other professional advisor) before using any of the suggested remedies, techniques, or information in this book.

Upon using the contents and information contained in this book, you agree to hold harmless the Author from and against any damages, costs, and expenses, including any legal fees potentially resulting from the application of any of the information provided by this book. This disclaimer applies to any loss, damages or injury caused by the use and application, whether directly or indirectly, of any advice or information presented, whether for breach of contract, tort, negligence, personal injury, criminal intent, or under any other cause of action. You agree to accept all risks of using the information presented inside this book.

You agree that by continuing to read this book, where appropriate and/or necessary, you shall consult a professional (including but not limited to your doctor, attorney, or financial advisor or such other advisor as needed) before using any of the suggested remedies, techniques, or information in this book.

TABLE OF CONTENT

DESCRIPTION

People always seek diets that'll assist them to support a healthy body and fit figure, but that'll also hold them full. Finding an excellent diet that offers healthy and tasty foods sometimes can be a challenge, particularly if you wish to lose some weight.

A Flexitarian diet has been trending lately. People are switching to this diet to improve their health, lose weight, and take care of the environment. In addition to improving health, this diet is more ethical. It is also more efficient because it uses less food and produces less waste. Consequently, switching to a vegetarian diet can benefit your body, the planet, and your wallet.

The benefits of going vegetarian are numerous, as it promotes good health and lowers cholesterol. It is also good for the environment because it reduces deforestation. People who go vegetarian have better eyesight because they do not consume excessive amounts of omega-6 fatty acids. This reduces inflammation in the eyes and promotes healthier vision.

It's a number coincidence that the title of the method is derived from the word «flexible. The zest of the approach is flexibility in relation to products of animal origin. In fact, the method is aimed at detoxifying the body's animal protein, as well as chemically processed foods and sugar.

Flexitarianism is based on eating more natural, biological, and healthy foods. Predominantly whole foods. However, when I wish for meat, I'm pleased to eat it. It's necessary not to overdo it and to purchase only quality, biological meat (number growth hormones or other artificial influences).

I hope I got your interest so far. If you're looking for a healthy way to modify your eating patterns and become more compassionate with every sentient being, let me guide you into the first chapter.

WHAT IS FLEXITARIAN DIET?

Today there is a wide range of dietary principles for all tastes and lifestyles. These include the «vegan» diet, which excludes all poultry, seafood, and meat, and the more strict vegan diet, which also excludes dairy products. But what about those who can't live without these nutritious protein foods? The new trend called «flexitarianism» should come to the aid of meat-eaters.

Most Americans do not consume the recommended amounts of dairy, fruits, legumes, seafood, whole grains, and other healthy foods. While it may seem daunting to completely overhaul your diet, one style of eating, the «flexitarian diet,» tries to make your food choices easier by focusing on «what to add» rather than «what to take.

Flexitarianism is a conflation of two words: «flexible» and «vegetarian. Although there is no single definition, flexitarianism is usually defined as semi-vegetarianism, including dairy products and eggs, with the occasional consumption of meat. It is believed that an emphasis on plant foods enhances the health benefits associated with a vegetarian diet without requiring the dietary restrictions inherent in a 100% vegetarian diet.

The Flexitarian diet does not set a target number of calories. Instead, the goal is to gradually increase the consumption of plant foods and products of plant origin, while not forgetting to reduce the frequency and quantity of meat and other products, although meat and other products are not forbidden.

Calories in the Flexitarian diet come mainly from nutritious foods such as fruits, legumes, and vegetables. For protein, the main source is plant foods (e.g. soy products, legumes, and nuts). Protein is also obtained from eggs and dairy products, and to a lesser extent from meat, especially red meat. Because of the emphasis on nutritious foods, it is recommended that the vegetarian diet should limit the consumption of saturated fats, sugar, and sodium.

Do not be afraid of this diet, you can eat vegetarian pizza, drink carbonated drinks and eat your favorite sweets. However, if you want to lose weight, you need to be careful about the quality of vegetarian food. Eat more fruits and vegetables and avoid processed foods. You need to replace saturated and trans fats with healthy fats (avocados, nuts, olive oil). Finally, if you want to lose weight in a healthy way, you need to burn calories and do physical exercise. For this, you need to change your eating habits and pay attention to the foods you eat, no matter how old you are. If weight loss and a healthy lifestyle are your main goals, a Flexitarian diet will do the job perfectly.

WHY YOU NEED TO START THE FLEXITARIAN DIET?

I want to tell you about how a plant-based diet can improve your health and lifestyle. If you compare two people, one a meat-eater and the other a flexitarian, the flexitarian tends to consume less saturated, overweight foods and cholesterol-raising foods. The flexitarian also gets more vitamins, as well as folic acid, potassium, dietary fiber, magnesium, and phytochemicals, among others. Thanks to the Flexitarian diet, flexitarians are more likely to have lower cholesterol and blood pressure levels as well as lower BMI (Body Mass Index). These three measures are associated with the risk of chronic disease as well as longevity.

However, it is important to note that eating healthy plant foods is not the only thing that will allow you to live a healthy lifestyle. It is also very important to exercise regularly, lives a stress-free life, quit smoking and drinking, and be psychologically healthy.

Adopting whole foods, plant-based diet will not only benefit your waistline but can also reduce the risk and symptoms of some chronic diseases. Here's what we know from medical research to date:

Heart Disease

Flexitarians have a lower risk of cardiac diseases (mainly heart attacks) and death from heart failures. Eating more plant-based foods through a Flexitarian diet may reduce one's risk for cardiovascular disease. Research has shown that a diet comprised predominantly of plant-based foods, such as fruits, vegetables, legumes, and nuts is associated with a lower risk of CVD. If you want to keep your heart in good health, the best thing is to eat whole-grain foods and legumes (high in fiber). Such foods keep the blood sugar levels in balance and reduce the levels of cholesterol.

Diabetes

Because it focuses on fresh ingredients and it packs plenty of vitamins, antioxidants, and minerals, this diet is a great way to keep your diabetes under control. This lifestyle controls excess insulin, which in turn lowers our blood sugar levels.

Regulating blood sugar levels is vastly important to living a healthier lifestyle. There is a need for balancing a lot of whole foods into this plan to find quality sources of protein and consume carbs that are low in sugar. That makes the body burn fat much more efficiently, and you will have more energy as a result. In short, a natural diet with fresh produce is a natural combater of diabetes.

Cancer

Flexitarian diet patterns have been associated with reduced risk of certain types of cancer, including colon cancer. According to the Oxford Vegetarian Study and EPIC-Oxford, fish-eaters had a lower risk of certain cancers than vegetarians who don't consume fish at all.

Weight Management

Although the main focus of this diet is not weight loss, it will surely help with it if that's what you're looking for. Just look at it from this point of view: fresh, clean food combined with whole grains, good fats, less sugar, and plenty of liquids coupled with copious amounts of exercise. By transitioning to healthy foods and a healthy lifestyle, you'll shed pounds without causing drastic imbalances in your body. Also, it is known that plant-based diets like the Flexitarian diet are really helpful in losing weight. The mere fact that you stopped eating junk food and processed food with sugar and unhealthy fats is already a very good start to weight loss!

Enhance Your Mood

The diet can help you to be positive, even when things aren't going your way. Healthy living does that. When you have eaten enough food to fuel you with lots of nutrients, your body notices. Fulfillment and productivity enhance your mood. For one, applying the diet correctly will make you feel like you're doing something good for yourself and thus enhances your overall mood.

Improve Skin Condition

Fish have Omega-3 fatty acids. They strengthen the skin membrane and make it more elastic and firmer. Olive oil, red wine, and tomatoes contain a lot of antioxidants to protect against skin damage brought about by chemical reactions and prolonged sun exposure.

Boost Brain Power

The Flexitarian diet can also counteract the brain's poor ability to perform. Choosing this lifestyle will actually help you preserve your memory, leading to an overall increase in your cognitive health.

Normally cognitive disorders are caused by a scenario where your brain is unable to get a sufficient amount of dopamine.

Dopamine is a compound or chemical present in the brain responsible for passing information from one neuron to the other. It is responsible for thought processing, mood regulation, and proper body movements.

The ability of this diet to help boost your cognitive health is normally linked to the combination of its anti-inflammatory fruits and vegetables, its healthy fats, and nuts.

These foods normally battle cognitive decline that is caused by age. But how do these foods do it? These foods normally deal with elements that cause impaired brain function like inflammation, free radicals, and exposure to toxicity.

Fatty fish, nuts, and olive oils all contain omega-3 fatty acids that usually help reduce the level of inflammation in your body. Such vegetables like spinach, kale, and broccoli that are dark green contain vitamin E, which is known to protect your body from an anti-inflammatory molecule known as cytokines.

Vegetables like spinach, broccoli, and fruits like raspberries, cherries, and watermelon all have antioxidants that neutralize free radicals that affect your brain. The Flexitarian diet also tends to focus on monounsaturated fats, which come from oils like olive oil. The oils and the fatty acids that you get from omega 3 (from fish) combine to keep your arteries unblocked.

That automatically increases the health of your brain and reduces your risk of getting diseases like Alzheimer's disease and dementia.

FLEXITARIAN DIET AND NO RULES

The Flexitarian diet is rich in whole foods and completely eliminates everything refined. Experts also recommend eliminating from your diet foods containing various «oriental» and components with hard-to-pronounce names.

Give preference to normal, healthy foods. The Flexitarian diet involves minimal consumption of dairy products, giving preference to sheep and goat products (necessarily organic, grown on farms). You can completely refuse cow's milk because of the hormones and antibiotics it contains in large quantities. Eat meat as you wish. Sometimes it is once a month, sometimes once a week, and sometimes you can eat it every day, just feel your body and desire. In the winter, for example, my body demands a great steak, and in the summer I don't even think about it.

Flexitarianism has a number of strict prohibitions because every «can't» is followed by a breakdown, psychological discomfort, and stress. That's the beauty of this diet - we can get all the necessary substances with our diet and not deprive ourselves of our favorite foods.

The main principles of Flexitarianism are to respect the proportions and precise combination of products, to choose products of excellent quality, and to listen to the needs of our bodies. In this way, your digestive system will always be in perfect order. Remember that food should not be a stress for you. Food should bring you health, joy, and pleasure.

Do not build for yourself unnecessary walls and prohibitions, eat in accordance with your intuition. There is no need to count the calories and weigh the food. It's enough to put the right emphasis. Do you want meat? Knock yourself out. It's all about balance. And you'll be happy.

FOODS TO EAT AND AVOID

You Can Eat:

All vegetables, including greens like spinach, kale, collards, asparagus, broccoli, bell peppers, tomatoes, onion, etc.

All fruits, including berries, avocados, apples, bananas, watermelons, grapes, oranges, etc.

Plant-based alternates to meat like tofu and tempeh.

Plant-based milk and dairy products including coconut milk, almond milk, peanut butter, almond butter, cashew yogurt, etc.

All whole-grains, including brown rice, amaranth, quinoa, all beans, whole wheat pasta, whole-grain bread, etc.

All nuts, including cashews, almonds, walnuts, etc.

All seeds like chia seeds, flaxseed, hempseeds, etc.

Lentils and millets.

Herbs, spices and seasonings: basil, oregano, mint, cumin, turmeric, ginger.

Condiments: low-sodium soy sauce, apple cider vinegar, salsa, yeast, ketchup without added sugar.

Drinks: still and sparkling water, tea, coffee.

When adding animal products, choose the following if possible:

○ Eggs: free-range or pasture-based.

○ Poultry: organic, free-range or pasture-raised.

○ Fish and seafood.

○ Meat: grass-fed or pasture-raised.

○ Dairy: organic from herbivorous or pasture-raised animals.

Foods You Should Avoid:

○ Fast food: cheeseburgers, hot dogs, chicken nuggets, etc.

○ Added sugars and sweets: sugar, soda, pastries, cookies, candy, etc.

○ Packaged and convenience foods: Chips, crackers, frozen dinners, etc.

○ Processed vegan-friendly foods

○ Processed animal products: Bacon, beef jerky, etc.

WILL THIS DIET HELP YOU LOSE WEIGHT?

The average person on a vegetarian diet may weigh less than those who regularly eat meat and animal products. This is due to the high protein and low-fat content of animal products.

Losing weight is an important motivator for many people when transitioning to a new diet. Not only does it make them feel better, but it can also improve their health.

Plant-based diets tend to be less caloric and rich in protein, which makes them great for weight loss. People who follow these diets can also have lower cholesterol levels because of their higher fiber content; this makes them great for treating obesity and other conditions associated with excessive blood cholesterol levels.

It's no coincidence that obesity is increasing at the same time that highly processed foods have become available. Processed foods can slow weight loss in several ways.

For instance, a diet of processed foods that don't provide enough iron could affect your ability to exercise, since iron is required to move oxygen around your body. This would limit your ability to burn calories through exercise.

Low-nutrient diets can also interfere with weight loss because people feel less fatigued after eating.

One study of 786 participants compared the fatness of participants who followed a low-nutrient diet to a high-nutrient diet.

After following the high micronutrient diet, about 80% of the participants felt more obese, even though they consumed fewer calories than the low micronutrient diet.

When trying to increase your nutrient intake, it is best to eat real foods, which contain many nutrients such as minerals, vitamins, and minerals that are not easily obtained from supplements.

Moreover, the nutrients in whole foods interact better with each other and are absorbed better than in supplements.

24

If you are interested in applying the Flexitarian diet to your life to lose weight, then these general dieting tips paired with this diet eating habits will help you maximize your weight loss.

Eat Slowly

It takes twenty minutes for your food to start digesting and give you a feeling of fullness after you eat a meal. Therefore, slow down and chew your food so that you can actually taste it and enjoy the flavor. If you tend to eat fast, you may find that you eat more because it takes that twenty minutes to get your internal system fired up.

Drink Water Before Your Meal

Try drinking a full eight-ounce glass of water before you sit down to eat a meal. Sometimes thirst can be mistaken for a feeling of hunger. Drinking a glass of water before you eat can get the digestion process started quicker, which can cause you to eat less during a meal.

Exercise

Adhere to the most foundational level, which is a daily activity. Do your best to get thirty minutes of exercise every day.

Adapt to Using Healthy Oil

When on a Flexitarian diet, fats are very important. But ensure you are ingesting the correct ones by using natural oils instead of butter.

Change the Way You Think About Food

See vegetables and fruits as snacks. Slice your vegetables into ready-to-eat snack sizes and wash your fruits when you bring them home from the store so that they are ready to grab as a quick snack when you're feeling hungry.

Always have a jar of mixed nuts within your reach on the kitchen counter and eat a handful of those along with your vegetable or fruit snack.

Prepackaged Snacks

Prepackaged snacks into portion sizes rather than eating from the full container. This can prevent overeating.

When you pre-allocate how much of a snack you're going to eat, then you're helping yourself stay disciplined.

Snack Two or Three Times a Day

Enjoy two or three snacking times a day where you eat a serving of fruit or vegetables with no salt or sugar added. Schedule a snack in the morning, afternoon, and before bed.

Learn a Well-Balanced Eating Plan

The longer you adhere to the Flexitarian diet, the more energy and vitality you will receive.

The Flexitarian diet offers a well-balanced eating plan that includes the correct amount of each food group.

30 DAYS MEAL PLAN

day 1
Breakfast: Strawberry Yogurt
Lunch: Quinoa Salad
Dinner: Avocado Salmon Salad
Snack/Dessert: Zucchini Dip

day 2
Breakfast: Edamame & Sweet Pea Hummus
Lunch: Mushroom Soup
Dinner: Cabbage And Chicken Mix
Snack/Dessert: Avocado Slices

day 3
Breakfast: Blueberry Pancakes
Lunch: Radish Cucumber Salad
Dinner: Cumin Salmon
Snack/Dessert: Chocolate Mousse

day 4
Breakfast: Tomatoes And Eggs
Lunch: Sweet Potato And White Bean Skillet
Dinner: Garlic Shrimp
Snack/Dessert: Fried Mushrooms

day 5
Breakfast: Tofu Scramble Toast
Lunch: Baked Vegetables
Dinner: Baked Chicken With Sweet Paprika
Snack/Dessert: Kale And Almonds

day 6
Breakfast: Hash Browns And Veggies
Lunch: Super Green Soup
Dinner: Seared Salmon And White Beans
Snack/Dessert: Orange Smoothie

day 7
Breakfast: Banana Strawberry Oats
Lunch: Broccoli And Tofu
Dinner: Chicken And Veggies Tortilla Soup
Snack/Dessert: Marinated Olives

day 8
Breakfast: Salmon Toast
Lunch: Coconut Chickpea Curry
Dinner: Grilled Corn
Snack/Dessert: Vegan Panna Cotta

day 9
Breakfast: Easy Breakfast Tacos
Lunch: Cauliflower Steak With Sweet-Pea Puree
Dinner: Ginger Halibut
Snack/Dessert: Delicious Hummus

day 10
Breakfast: Raspberry Shake
Lunch: Chickpea And Spinach Cutlets
Dinner: Radish Salmon Salad
Snack/Dessert: Cauliflower Popcorn

day 11
Breakfast: Edamame & Sweet Pea Hummus
Lunch: Italian Tomato Soup
Dinner: Turkey Meatballs With Tomato Sauce
Snack/Dessert: Avocado Slices

day 12
Breakfast: Granola With Grapefruit
Lunch: Black Bean And Quinoa Salad
Dinner: Shrimp Zoodles
Snack/Dessert: Chocolate Mousse

day 13
Breakfast: Green Eggs
Lunch: Mushroom Soup
Dinner: Spinach With Garbanzo Beans
Snack/Dessert: Kale And Almonds

day 14
Breakfast: Chia Seed Pudding
Lunch: Grilled Corn
Dinner: Cabbage And Chicken Mix
Snack/Dessert: Marinated Olives

day 15
Breakfast: Hash Browns And Veggies
Lunch: Cauliflower And Green Beans
Dinner: Garlic Shrimp
Snack/Dessert: Fried Mushrooms

day 16
Breakfast: Tomatoes And Eggs
Lunch: Vegetable Wraps
Dinner: Chicken In Tomato Sauce
Snack/Dessert: Orange Smoothie

day 17
Breakfast: Veggie Breakfast Bowl
Lunch: Avocado Soup
Dinner: Fish Tacos
Snack/Dessert: Vegan Panna Cotta

day 18
Breakfast: Banana Strawberry Oats
Lunch: Radish Cucumber Salad
Dinner: Sea Bass
Snack/Dessert: Delicious Hummus

day 19
Breakfast: Avocado Spread
Lunch: Baked Broccoli
Dinner: Cumin Salmon
Snack/Dessert: Zucchini Dip

day 20
Breakfast: Strawberry Yogurt
Lunch: Coconut Chickpea Curry
Dinner: Teriyaki Chicken
Snack/Dessert: Avocado Slices

day 21
Breakfast: Tofu Scramble Toast
Lunch: Italian Tomato Soup
Dinner: Chicken Pieces
Snack/Dessert: Fried Mushrooms

day 22
Breakfast: Blueberry Pancakes
Lunch: Quinoa With Acorn Squash & Swiss Chard
Dinner: Avocado Salmon Salad
Snack/Dessert: Cauliflower Popcorn

day 23
Breakfast: Granola For Breakfast
Lunch: Sweet Potato And White Bean Skillet
Dinner: Baked Salmon With Lemon
Snack/Dessert: Marinated Olives

day 24
Breakfast: Easy Breakfast Tacos
Lunch: Cauliflower And Green Beans
Dinner: Shrimp Zoodles
Snack/Dessert: Delicious Hummus

day 25
Breakfast: Chia Seed Pudding
Lunch: Chickpea And Spinach Cutlets
Dinner: Ginger Halibut
Snack/Dessert: Vegan Panna Cotta

day 26
Breakfast: Raspberry Shake
Lunch: Zucchini Cakes
Dinner: Delicious Salmon
Snack/Dessert: Chocolate Mousse

day 27
Breakfast: Green Eggs
Lunch: Black Bean And Quinoa Salad
Dinner: Fish Tacos
Snack/Dessert: Kale And Almonds

day 28
Breakfast: Veggie Breakfast Bowl
Lunch: Avocado Soup
Dinner: Chicken Couscous
Snack/Dessert: Orange Smoothie

day 29
Breakfast: Avocado Spread
Lunch: Cauliflower Steak With Sweet-Pea Puree
Dinner: Baked Salmon With Lemon
Snack/Dessert: Zucchini Dip

day 30
Breakfast: Granola With Grapefruit
Lunch: Broccoli And Tofu
Dinner: Sea Bass
Snack/Dessert: Marinated Olives

41

BREAKFAST RECIPES

BANANA STRAWBERRY OATS

 Cooking Difficulty: 1/10

 Cooking Time: 15 minutes

 Servings: 1

INGREDIENTS

- 1 tbsp. sliced almonds
- ½ c. oats
- ½ tsp. cinnamon
- 1 c. shredded zucchini
- ½ banana, mashed
- 1 c. water
- ½ c. sliced strawberries
- dash of salt
- 1 tbsp. flax meal

DESCRIPTION

STEP 1
First, combine oats, salt, water, and zucchini in a large saucepan.

STEP 2
Cook the mixture over medium-high heat and cook for 8 to 10 minutes or until the liquid is absorbed.

STEP 3
Now, spoon in all the remaining ingredients to the mixture and give everything a good stir.

STEP 4
Finally, transfer the mixture to a serving bowl and top it with almonds and strawberries. Serve and enjoy.

NUTRITIONAL INFORMATION

Calories: 386, Proteins: 23.7g, Carbs: 57.5g, Fat: 8.9g

EDAMAME & SWEET PEA HUMMUS

 Cooking Difficulty:
1/10

 Cooking Time:
5 minutes

 Servings:
2

INGREDIENTS

- ½ c. edamame
- ½ c. peas
- 2 tbsps. tahini
- 1 minced garlic clove
- 2 tbsps. chopped mint
- 3 tbsps. olive oil
- 2 wheat tortillas
- 2 eggs

DESCRIPTION

STEP 1
Blend the first 5 ingredients and 1 Tbsp. Of olive oil in a food processor. Spread evenly over the wheat tortillas.

STEP 2
Coat the pan with the remaining olive oil and cook the eggs. When ready, put one egg on each tortilla.

NUTRITIONAL INFORMATION

15g Carbs, 10g Fat, 10g Protein, 260 Calories

47

GRANOLA WITH GRAPEFRUIT

 Cooking Difficulty: 1/10

 Cooking Time: 3 minutes

 Servings: 2

INGREDIENTS

- 1/2 cup coconut cream
- 6 tbsp. granola
- grapefruit

DESCRIPTION

STEP 1
Take two cups. Place 3 spoonfuls of granola in each one.

STEP 2
Then place the coconut cream on top of the granola.

STEP 3
Garnish everything with grapefruit. Enjoy your meal.

NUTRITIONAL INFORMATION

111 Calories, 6g Fats, 3g Carbs, 6.8 Protein

TOMATOES AND EGGS

 Cooking Difficulty: 2/10

 Cooking Time: 15 minutes

 Servings: 2

INGREDIENTS

- 1 tbsp. olive oil
- salt
- black pepper
- dried basil
- 1 tbsp. chopped parsley
- 4 eggs
- 6 tomatoes diced

DESCRIPTION

STEP 1
Heat olive oil in a pan.

STEP 2
Add tomatoes, spices, and herbs. Simmer, stirring, for about 5-7 minutes.

STEP 3
Make small wells in the sauce and break the eggs into them. Season with salt and cook until the white is white and the yolk inside is still runny.

STEP 4
Remove from fire. Sprinkle with parsley before serving.

NUTRITIONAL INFORMATION

Calories: 180, Fat: 4 g, Carbs: 5 g, Protein: 3 g

EASY BREAKFAST TACOS

 Cooking Difficulty: 3/10	Cooking Time: 11 minutes	Servings: 2

NUTRITIONAL INFORMATION

299 Calories, 7g Fats, 6g Carbs, 6g Protein

INGREDIENTS

- 2 low carb tortillas
- 4 large eggs
- ½ sliced avocado
- 2 tbsps. mayonnaise (optional)
- 1 tbsp. olive oil
- 4 fresh cilantro sprigs
- tabasco sauce
- sea salt
- black pepper

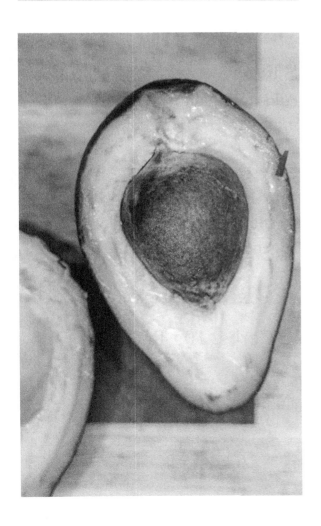

DESCRIPTION

STEP 1

Whisk the eggs in a bowl until smooth. Set aside. Place a nonstick skillet over medium flame and heat through. Once hot, add the olive oil and swirl to coat.

STEP 2

Add the egg and tilt until the eggs are spread out. Cook until done, then transfer to a bowl. Set aside.

STEP 3

Warm the tortillas over a low flame, then place on a platter and spread the mayonnaise on one side of each tortilla.

STEP 4

Divide the egg between the two tortillas, then add the sliced avocado, and cilantro. Season with salt and pepper, then add the pepper sauce. Roll up the tortillas and serve.

TOFU SCRAMBLE TOAST

 Cooking Difficulty: 2/10

 Cooking Time: 7 minutes

 Servings: 2

INGREDIENTS

- 14 ounces of drained and diced tofu
- ½ yellow onion
- 2 teaspoons cajun seasoning
- 2 toasted bread
- favorite vegetables for serving

DESCRIPTION

STEP 1
Heat a frying pan and add a little olive oil.

STEP 2
Add tofu and spices. Cook for 5 minutes.

STEP 3
Fry one side of the toast. Place tofu on toast. Garnish with your favorite vegetables. Serve for breakfast.

NUTRITIONAL INFORMATION

247 Calories, 5.8g Fats, 6g Carbs, 10g Protein

RASPBERRY SHAKE

 Cooking Difficulty: 1/10

 Cooking Time: 1 minutes

 Servings: 2

INGREDIENTS

- 1 c. raspberries
- 2 c. almond milk
- cashew nuts
- 1 tsp. vanilla extract

DESCRIPTION

STEP 1
Using a blender, set in all your ingredients and blend until very smooth. Enjoy.

NUTRITIONAL INFORMATION

Calories: 185, Fat: 8.9 g, Carbs: 2.3 g, Protein: 4 g

GREEN EGGS

 Cooking Difficulty: 2/10

 Cooking Time: 9 minutes

 Servings: 2

INGREDIENTS

- ¼ tsp. ground cayenne
- ¼ tsp. ground cumin
- 4 eggs
- ½ c. chopped parsley
- ½ c. chopped cilantro
- 1 tsp. thyme leaves
- 2 garlic cloves
- 2 tbsp. olive oil

DESCRIPTION

STEP 1
Olive oil in a skillet before adding the garlic and frying.

STEP 2
Add in the thyme, parsley, and cilantro and cook another 3 minutes.

STEP 3
At this time, add in the eggs and season. Cover with a lid and let this cook for another 5 minutes before serving.

NUTRITIONAL INFORMATION

311 Calories, 27g Fats, 4g Carbs, 12.8 Protein

59

CHIA SEED PUDDING

 Cooking Difficulty:
1/10

 Cooking Time:
12 minutes

 Servings:
1

INGREDIENTS

- 1/2 cup coconut milk
- 2 tbsp. chia seeds
- berries

DESCRIPTION

STEP 1
Combine chia seeds and milk in a large bowl. Let the mixture sit for 10 minutes, then stir again as soon as the chia seeds begin to swell.

STEP 2
Cover the bowl with a lid and refrigerate for an hour or more.

STEP 3
Stir the chia pudding before serving and add your favorite berries. Enjoy!

NUTRITIONAL INFORMATION

180 Calories, 3 g Fat, 3g Carbs, 3g Protein

61

STRAWBERRY YOGURT

 Cooking Difficulty: 1/10	Cooking Time: 10 minutes	Servings: 2

INGREDIENTS

- 1 c. strawberry halved
- 2 c. yogurt

DESCRIPTION

STEP 1
In a bowl, combine the yogurt with the strawberry, and toss and keep in the fridge for 10 minutes.

STEP 2
Divide into bowls and serve breakfast.

NUTRITIONAL INFORMATION

Calories: 79, Fat: 0.4 g, Carbs: 15 g, Protein: 1.3 g

BLUEBERRY PANCAKES

 Cooking Difficulty: 3/10

 Cooking Time: 32 minutes

 Servings: 10

INGREDIENTS

- 1 tbsp. olive oil
- 1 c. yogurt, full-fat
- ½ tsp. vanilla extract
- 4 tbsps. almond milk
- 1 ½ c. almond flour
- 1 c. blueberries
- 2 eggs, whisked
- 3 tbsps. coconut butter, melted

DESCRIPTION

STEP 1
In a bowl, combine the eggs with the almond milk and the other ingredients except the oil and whisk well.

STEP 2
Heat up a pan with the oil over medium heat, add ¼ cup of the batter, spread into the pan, cook for 4 minutes, flip, cook for 3 minutes more and transfer to a plate.

STEP 3
Repeat with the rest of the batter and serve the pancakes for breakfast.

NUTRITIONAL INFORMATION

Calories 64, Fat 4.4g, Carbs 4.7g, Protein 1.8g

AVOCADO SPREAD

 Cooking Difficulty: 1/10

 Cooking Time: 1 minutes

 Servings: 4

INGREDIENTS

- 3 peeled and pitted avocados, chopped
- 1 tbsp. olive oil
- 1 tbsp. lime juice
- salt
- black pepper
- 1 tbsp. chopped chives
- 4 eggs

DESCRIPTION

STEP 1
In a blender, mix the avocado pulp with oil and other ingredients.

STEP 2
Heat a skillet over low heat and add olive oil. Fry eggs until done.

STEP 3
Spread guacamole on bread and top with a fried egg.

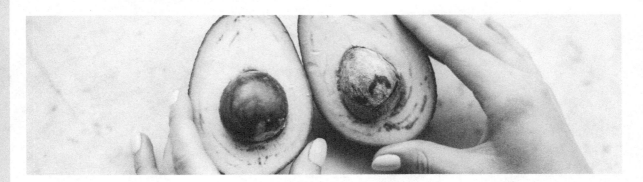

NUTRITIONAL INFORMATION

Calories: 79, Fat: 0.4 g, Carbs: 15 g, Protein: 1.3 g

HASH BROWNS AND VEGGIES

 Cooking Difficulty:
3/10

 Cooking Time:
23 minutes

Servings:
4

INGREDIENTS

- 1 tbsp. cilantro, chopped
- 4 eggs, whisked
- ¼ tsp. black pepper
- 1 c. hash browns
- 1 onion, small and chopped
- ½ bell pepper, chopped
- 1 tbsp. olive oil
- ½ red bell pepper, chopped

DESCRIPTION

STEP 1
Heat up a pan with the oil over medium-high heat, add the onion and the hash browns and cook for 5 minutes.

STEP 2
Add the bell peppers and cook for 5 minutes more.

STEP 3
Add the eggs, and black pepper, and stir and cook for another 10 minutes.

STEP 4
Add the cilantro, stir, cook for a couple more seconds, divide everything between plates, and serve for breakfast.

NUTRITIONAL INFORMATION

311 Calories, 27g Fats, 4g Carbs, 12.8 Protein

69

SALMON TOAST

 Cooking Difficulty: 1/10

 Cooking Time: 3 minutes

 Servings: 2

INGREDIENTS

- lightly salted salmon
- 1 cucumber
- vegan cream cheese
- 4 toasted bread slices

DESCRIPTION

STEP 1
Slice the cucumber into slices.

STEP 2
Spread cream cheese on toasted bread. Place lightly salted salmon on top.

STEP 3
Garnish with microgreen, if desired. Enjoy your meal.

NUTRITIONAL INFORMATION

Calories: 210, Fat: 4.4 g, Carbs: 3.8 g, Protein: 6 g

VEGGIE BREAKFAST BOWL

 Cooking Difficulty: 2/10

 Cooking Time: 5 minutes

 Servings: 1

INGREDIENTS

- 1 egg
- 1 tbsp. water
- 2 tbsps. diced mushrooms
- ¼ c. baby spinach
- 2 tbsps. cherry tomatoes

DESCRIPTION

STEP 1
Mix all ingredients in a greased microwaveable bowl.

STEP 2
Microwave for 1 minute or until the egg is cooked.

NUTRITIONAL INFORMATION

2g Carbs, 6g Fat, 10g Protein, 100 Calories

GRANOLA FOR BREAKFAST

 Cooking Difficulty:
1/10

 Cooking Time:
3 minutes

 Servings:
2

INGREDIENTS

- 1/2 cup coconut cream
- 6 tbsp. granola
- strawberries

DESCRIPTION

STEP 1
Take two cups. Place 3 spoonfuls of granola in each one.

STEP 2
Then place the coconut cream on top of the granola.

STEP 3
Garnish everything with the strawberries. Enjoy your meal.

NUTRITIONAL INFORMATION

211 Calories, 17g Fats, 6g Carbs, 9.8 Protein

VEGETABLES

ITALIAN TOMATO SOUP

 Cooking Difficulty: 2/10	Cooking Time: 25 minutes	Servings: 3

INGREDIENTS

- 1 pound tomatoes
- 3 cloves of garlic
- 3 cups vegetable broth
- 2 tbsp. olive oil
- 1 green basil, bundle
- dry bread (optional)
- sea salt
- black pepper

DESCRIPTION

STEP 1
Heat olive oil in a large saucepan over medium heat. Add the garlic and fry for 1 minute.

STEP 2
In a separate bowl, chop the tomatoes. Place them in the pan. Season with salt and pepper. Partially cover and stew over medium heat for about ten minutes. Add the broth and basil, return to the stove and simmer for another ten minutes. Add the bread cubes and stew for another ten minutes until the bread is soft.

STEP 3
Serve with extra olive oil and put in more fresh basil!

NUTRITIONAL INFORMATION

110 Calories, 2g Fats, 3g Carbs, and 3g Protein

CHICKPEA AND SPINACH CUTLETS

 Cooking Difficulty: 3/10	Cooking Time: 40 minutes	Servings: 12

NUTRITIONAL INFORMATION

170 Calories, 5g Fat, 1.7g Carbs, 4g Protein

INGREDIENTS

- 1 red bell pepper
- 19 oz. chickpeas, rinsed & drained
- 1 c. ground almonds
- 2 tsps. dijon mustard
- 1 tsp. oregano
- 1 c. spinach, fresh
- 1½ c. rolled oats
- 1 clove garlic, pressed
- ½ lemon, juiced

DESCRIPTION

STEP 1
Get out a baking sheet. Line it with parchment paper.

STEP 2
Cut your red pepper in half and then take the seeds out. Place it on your baking sheet, and roast it in the oven while you prepare your other ingredients.

STEP 3
Process your chickpeas, almonds, and mustard together in a food processor.

STEP 4
Add in your lemon juice, oregano, sage, garlic, and spinach, processing again. Make sure it's combined, but don't puree it.

STEP 5
Once your red bell pepper is softened, which should roughly take ten minutes, add this to the processor as well. Add in your oats, mixing well.

STEP 6
Form twelve patties, cooking in the oven for a half hour. They should be browned.

ZUCCHINI CAKES

 Cooking Difficulty: 2/10

 Cooking Time: 22 minutes

 Servings: 4

INGREDIENTS

- 2 tbsps. olive oil
- 2 tbsps. almond flour
- 1/3 c. carrot, shredded
- 1 tsp. lemon zest, grated
- 1 garlic clove, minced
- 1 egg, whisked
- 2 zucchinis, grated
- 1 yellow onion, chopped
- black pepper
- sea salt

DESCRIPTION

STEP 1

In a bowl, combine the zucchinis with the garlic, onion, and the other ingredients except for the oil, stir well and shape medium cakes out of this mix.

STEP 2

Heat up a pan with the oil over medium-high heat, add the zucchini cakes, cook for 5 minutes on each side, divide between plates and serve with a side salad.

NUTRITIONAL INFORMATION

Calories 271, Fat 8.7g, Carbs 14.3g, Protein 4.6g

VEGETABLE WRAPS

 Cooking Difficulty: 2/10

 Cooking Time: 9 minutes

 Servings: 4

INGREDIENTS

- 1 head of romaine lettuce
- 2 carrots
- 1 cucumber
- 1 red onion
- 1 celery stalk
- dressing of choice

DESCRIPTION

STEP 1
Finely slice the carrots, cucumber, red onion, and celery into sticks of vegetable.

STEP 2
Divide between 12 lettuce leaves.

STEP 3
Roll up lettuce leaves and serve.

NUTRITIONAL INFORMATION

20 Calories, 6g Fats, 1g Carbs, and 0g Protein

MUSHROOM SOUP

 Cooking Difficulty: 2/10

 Cooking Time: 20 minutes

 Servings: 2

INGREDIENTS

- 1 pound champignons
- 3 shallots
- 2 cloves of garlic
- 2 cups chicken broth
- 7 tbsp. natural yogurt
- 2 tbsp. olive oil

DESCRIPTION

STEP 1

Sauté the finely chopped onion in a saucepan in olive oil until tender.

STEP 2

Add mushrooms and garlic. Then pour chicken broth into a saucepan, bring to a boil and cook for another 10 minutes, until mushrooms are tender.

STEP 3

Whisk the soup with a blender and season with natural yogurt before serving.

NUTRITIONAL INFORMATION

201 Calories, 8.1g Fats, 3g Carbs, 3 Protein

COCONUT CHICKPEA CURRY

 Cooking Difficulty: 4/10

 Cooking Time: 27 minutes

 Servings: 4

NUTRITIONAL INFORMATION

Calories: 225, Fat: 9.4 g, Carbs: 28.5 g, Protein: 7.3

INGREDIENTS

- 2 tsps. coconut flour
- 16 oz. cooked chickpeas
- 14 oz. tomatoes, diced
- 1 onion, sliced
- 1 ½ tsps. minced garlic
- ½ tsp. salt
- 1 tsp. curry powder
- 1/3 tsp. ground black pepper
- ¼ tsp. cumin
- 1 lemon, juiced
- 13.5 oz. coconut milk, unsweetened
- 2 tbsps. coconut oil

DESCRIPTION

STEP 1

Take a large pot, place it over medium-high heat, add oil and when it melts, add onions and tomatoes, season with salt and black pepper and cook for 5 minutes.

STEP 2

Switch heat to medium-low level, cook for 10 minutes until tomatoes have released their liquid, then add chickpeas and stir in garlic, curry powder, and cumin until combined.

STEP 3

Stir in milk and flour, bring the mixture to boil, then switch heat to medium heat and simmer the curry for 12 minutes until cooked.

STEP 4

Taste to adjust seasoning, drizzle with lemon juice, and serve. Place remaining portions in an airtight container and refrigerate for up to 2 days. Reheat before serving.

BROCCOLI AND TOFU

 Cooking Difficulty: 3/10

 Cooking Time: 20 minutes

 Servings: 2

INGREDIENTS

- 1 head of broccoli
- tofu
- 1 clove of garlic
- 3 tsp soy sauce

DESCRIPTION

STEP 1
Cut broccoli flowers into small pieces.

STEP 2
Steam the broccoli for about 2 to 3 minutes, until tender. Remove from heat and dip broccoli in cold water, then transfer to a bowl and set aside.

STEP 3
Wrap the tofu in a paper towel and press lightly to remove excess liquid, then crush with a fork.

STEP 4
Finely chop the garlic, mix with the soy sauce, then add the tofu and stir gently. Top with broccoli and sauce and tofu.

NUTRITIONAL INFORMATION

190 Calories, 6g Protein, 7g Fat, 5,4g Carbs

QUINOA SALAD

 Cooking Difficulty: 3/10	Cooking Time: 20 minutes	Servings: 4

NUTRITIONAL INFORMATION

380 Calories, 26g Fats, 5g Carbs, 8g Protein

INGREDIENTS

- 1 c. uncooked quinoa
- 1/3 c. red wine vinegar
- 2 c. water
- ¼ c. olive oil
- 1 red pepper, diced
- 1 red onion, diced
- ½ c. kalamata olives
- 1 juiced lemon
- ½ c. freshly chopped cilantro
- ½ tsp. black pepper
- 1 tsp. salt
- ½ c. crumbled feta cheese (optional)
- 2 roma tomatoes

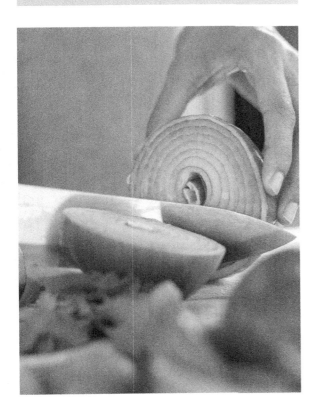

DESCRIPTION

STEP 1
First, you will need to dice the tomatoes, onions, and peppers.

STEP 2
Prepare a pot of water (med. heat) to boil, and add the quinoa. Reduce the heat and cook for 15-20 minutes. The water should be completely absorbed—fluff and cool for five minutes.

STEP 3
Add the vinegar and oil—as the quinoa comes to room temperature.

STEP 4
Blend in the tomatoes, onion, olives, red peppers, cilantro, pepper, and salt. Gently blend and add the feta cheese. Refrigerate for about two hours so the flavors can intertwine.

STEP 5
Before serving, give it a drizzle of lemon juice.

93

BAKED VEGETABLES

 Cooking Difficulty: 2/10

 Cooking Time: 35 minutes

 Servings: 2

INGREDIENTS

- 2 minced garlic cloves
- 2 tablespoons olive oil
- 1/2 pound broccoli florets
- 2 carrots
- green beans (optional)
- black pepper
- salt
- 2 eggs

DESCRIPTION

STEP 1
Slice the carrots into slices. In a roasting pan, combine the vegetables together with the oil, garlic and spices, toss and bake at 400 degrees F for 15 minutes.

STEP 2
When the time is up, take out the mold and pour the two eggs into it. Return to the oven and bake until the eggs are cooked.

STEP 3
Divide the mix between plates and serve.

NUTRITIONAL INFORMATION

260 Calories, 4.9g Protein, 7g Fat, 4,4g Carbs

SPINACH WITH GARBANZO BEANS

 Cooking Difficulty: 2/10

 Cooking Time: 8 minutes

 Servings: 4

INGREDIENTS

- 1 tbsp. olive oil
- 4 minced garlic cloves
- ½ diced onion
- 10 oz. chopped spinach
- 12 oz. garbanzo beans
- ½ tsp. cumin
- ½ tsp. salt

DESCRIPTION

STEP 1
In a skillet, warm the olive oil over medium-low heat.

STEP 2
Then add the onions and garlic and cook until the onions are translucent. About 5 minutes.

STEP 3
Stir in spinach, cumin, salt, and garbanzo beans.

STEP 4
Allow cooking until thoroughly heated.

NUTRITIONAL INFORMATION

90 Calories, 4g Fat, 11g Carbs, 4g Protein

97

BAKED BROCCOLI

 Cooking Difficulty: 2/10

 Cooking Time: 20 minutes

 Servings: 4

INGREDIENTS

- 2 minced garlic cloves
- 2 tbsps. olive oil
- 1 lb. broccoli florets
- ½ tsp. ground nutmeg
- black pepper

DESCRIPTION

STEP 1
In a roasting pan, combine the broccoli with the garlic and the other ingredients, toss and bake at 400 degrees F for 20 minutes.

STEP 2
Divide the mix between plates and serve.

NUTRITIONAL INFORMATION

165 Calories, 8g Fats, 7g Carbs, 7g Protein

CAULIFLOWER STEAK WITH SWEET-PEA PUREE

 Cooking Difficulty: 3/10

 Cooking Time: 35 minutes

 Servings: 2

NUTRITIONAL INFORMATION

Calories 234, Fat 3.8g, Carbs 40.3g, Protein 14.5g

INGREDIENTS

cauliflower:
- 2 heads cauliflower
- 1 tsp. olive oil
- ¼ tsp. paprika
- ¼ tsp. black pepper

sweet-pea puree:
- 10 oz. frozen green peas
- 1 onion, chopped
- 2 tbsps. fresh parsley
- ¼ c. unsweetened vegan milk

DESCRIPTION

STEP 1
Preheat oven to 425F.

STEP 2
Remove bottom core of cauliflower. Stand it on its base, starting in the middle, slice in half. Then slice steaks about ¾ inches thick.

STEP 3
Using a baking pan, set in the steaks.

STEP 4
Using olive oil, coat the front and back of the steaks.

STEP 5
Sprinkle with paprika, and pepper.

STEP 6
Bake for 30 minutes, flipping once.

STEP 7
Meanwhile, steam the chopped onion and peas until soft.

STEP 8
Place these vegetables in a blender with milk and parsley and blend until smooth.

RADISH CUCUMBER SALAD

 Cooking Difficulty:
1/10

 Cooking Time:
3 minutes

 Servings:
2

INGREDIENTS

- 8 radishes
- 2 cucumber
- olive oil
- salt
- lime slice
- 0.5 cup fresh green peas
- salad greens

DESCRIPTION

STEP 1
Slice the radish and cucumber. Mix all ingredients, top with a lime slice on the salad and garnish with herbs as desired.

NUTRITIONAL INFORMATION

60 Calories, 0,4g Fats, 0,6g Carbs, and 0,2g Protein

SWEET POTATO AND WHITE BEAN SKILLET

Cooking Difficulty: 4/10	Cooking Time: 30 minutes	Servings: 4

NUTRITIONAL INFORMATION

Calories: 260, Fat: 4 g, Carbs: 24 g, Protein: 13 g

INGREDIENTS

- 1 bunch kale, chopped
- 2 sweet potatoes, peeled, cubed
- 12 oz. cannellini beans
- 1 peeled onion, diced
- 1/8 tsp. red pepper flakes
- 1 tsp. salt
- ½ tsp. black pepper
- 1 tsp. curry powder
- 1 ½ tbsps. coconut oil
- 6 oz. coconut milk
- chickpeas (optional)

DESCRIPTION

STEP 1
Take a large skillet pan, place it over medium heat, add ½ tablespoon oil and when it melts, add onion and cook for 5 minutes.

STEP 2
Then stir in sweet potatoes, stir well, cook for 5 minutes, then season with all the spices, cook for 1 minute and remove the pan from heat.

STEP 3
Take another pan, add remaining oil in it, place it over medium heat and when oil melts, add kale, season with some salt and black pepper, stir well, pour in the milk and cook for 15 minutes until tender.

STEP 4
Then add beans, beans, and red pepper, stir until mixed and cook for 5 minutes until hot.

STEP 5
Serve straight away.

SUPER GREEN SOUP

 Cooking Difficulty: 2/10

 Cooking Time: 15 minutes

 Servings: 6

INGREDIENTS

- pepper
- salt
- ¼ c. coconut oil
- 1 c. coconut milk
- 4 c. vegetable stock
- 2 c. spinach
- 1 c. watercress
- 1 bay leaf
- 2 minced garlic cloves
- 1 chopped onion
- 1 chopped cauliflower head

DESCRIPTION

STEP 1
Grease up a pan with some oil and cook the garlic and onion. When those are browned, add the bay leaf and cauliflower and cook for another 5 minutes.

STEP 2
Add the spinach and watercress and cook for a bit to wilt. Pour in the vegetable stock and let this boil. Cook for another 8 minutes.

STEP 3
Add in the coconut milk and then remove it from the heat. Blend so this becomes smooth and creamy. This can be frozen or left in the fridge for five days.

NUTRITIONAL INFORMATION

192 Calories, 8g Fats, 7g Carbs, 7g Protein

BLACK BEAN AND QUINOA SALAD

Cooking Difficulty: 2/10	Cooking Time: 5 minutes	Servings: 10

INGREDIENTS

- 15 ounces boiled black beans
- 1 chopped red bell pepper without core
- 1 in. quinoa, cooked
- 1 green bell pepper, cored, chopped
- 5 ounces of canned corn
- parsley

DESCRIPTION

STEP 1
In a bowl, set in all ingredients, and stir until incorporated.

STEP 2
Top the salad with parsley and serve straight away. Place remaining portions in an airtight container and refrigerate for up to 4 days.

NUTRITIONAL INFORMATION

Calories: 64, Fat: 1 g, Carbs: 8 g, Protein: 3 g

AVOCADO SOUP

 Cooking Difficulty: 1/10

 Cooking Time: 5 minutes

 Servings: 4

INGREDIENTS

- 2 pcs. avocado
- ½ pack of arugula
- mint handful
- ⅓ glasses of coconut cream
- 3.5 cups water
- 1 pc. lemon juice
- 1 tbsp. olive oil
- salt pepper

DESCRIPTION

STEP 1
Combine all ingredients (except oil) in a blender at high speed until smooth.

STEP 2
Serve garnished with olive oil and a couple of mint leaves. This can be frozen or left in the fridge for 4 days.

NUTRITIONAL INFORMATION

365 Calories, 22g Fats, 7g Carbs, 7g Protein

QUINOA WITH ACORN SQUASH & SWISS CHARD

 Cooking Difficulty: 2/10

 Cooking Time: 7 minutes

 Servings: 4

INGREDIENTS

- ¾ c. canned acorn squash puree
- ½ tbsp. moroccan seasoning
- 1¾ c. uncooked quinoa, well rinsed
- ½ tsp. sea salt
- 2½ c. water
- ¼ tsp. ground allspice
- 1½ c. swiss chard, trimmed and torn into pieces

DESCRIPTION

STEP 1
Throw all the ingredients into the pot except for the Swiss chard.

STEP 2
Set the pot to Manual mode, on high, with a cook time of 5-minutes.

STEP 3
When the cooking time is completed, release the pressure using quick-release.

STEP 4
Add the Swiss chard and stir, serve right away.

NUTRITIONAL INFORMATION

Calories: 281, Fat: 4.6g, Carbs: 23g, Protein: 12.1g

113

CAULIFLOWER AND GREEN BEANS

Cooking Difficulty: 2/10	Cooking Time: 30 minutes	Servings: 4

INGREDIENTS

- 1 lb. cauliflower florets
- 1 tbsp. olive oil
- 2 minced garlic cloves
- 1 c. tomato pasta
- salt
- black pepper
- ½ lb. trimmed green beans halved
- 1 tbsp. chopped cilantro
- green peas optional

DESCRIPTION

STEP 1
Heat up a pot with the oil over medium-high heat; add the garlic and sauté for 3 minutes.

STEP 2
Add the cauliflower and the other ingredients, toss, then cook everything for 25 minutes more.

STEP 2
Divide everything between plates and serve.

NUTRITIONAL INFORMATION

Calories 93, Fat 3.7g, Carbs 13.7g, Protein 4.1g

GRILLED CORN

 Cooking Difficulty: 2/10

 Cooking Time: 15 minutes

 Servings: 2

INGREDIENTS

- 2 ears of corn
- 2 tablespoons of olive oil
- Salt and pepper to taste

DESCRIPTION

STEP 1

Preheat a grill or grill pan to medium-high heat. Remove the husks and silk from the corn. Rinse the corn with cold water and pat it dry with a paper towel. Brush the corn with olive oil and sprinkle with salt and pepper to taste.

STEP 2

Place the corn on the grill or grill pan, turning occasionally, until the corn is lightly charred on all sides and cooked through about 10-12 minutes.

STEP 3

Remove the corn from the grill and let it cool for a few minutes. Serve.

NUTRITIONAL INFORMATION

101 Calories, 1.1g Fats, 2g Carbs, 3 Protein

FISH & SEAFOOD

119

AVOCADO SALMON SALAD

 Cooking Difficulty:
1/10

 Cooking Time:
3 minutes

 Servings:
2

INGREDIENTS

- chopped lightly salted salmon
- 2 tbsp. avocado oil
- 2 sliced avocados
- 2 tbsp. lime juice
- 1 sliced cucumber
- black pepper
- favorite lettuce leaves if desired

DESCRIPTION

STEP 1

In a bowl, mix the avocado slices with the salmon and the rest of the ingredients, stir and serve for lunch.

NUTRITIONAL INFORMATION

Calories 200, Fat 10g, Carbs 3g, Protein 7g

121

SHRIMP ZOODLES

 Cooking Difficulty: 2/10	Cooking Time: 10 minutes	Servings: 4

NUTRITIONAL INFORMATION

277 Calories, 15.6g Fat, 5.9g Carbs, 7.5g Protein

INGREDIENTS

- 4 c. zoodles
- 1 tbsp. chopped basil
- 1 lb. shrimp
- 1 c. vegetable stock
- 2 minced garlic cloves
- 2 tbsps. olive oil
- ½ lemon
- ½ tsp. paprika

DESCRIPTION

STEP 1
Set your Instant Pot to SAUTÉ and add the olive oil in it.

STEP 2
Add garlic and cook for 1 minute.

STEP 3
Add the lemon juice and shrimp and cook for another minute.

STEP 4
Stir in the remaining ingredients and close the lid.

STEP 5
Set the Instant Pot to MANUAL and cook at low pressure for 5 minutes.

STEP 6
Do a quick pressure release.

STEP 7
Serve and enjoy!

CUMIN SALMON

 Cooking Difficulty: 2/10

 Cooking Time: 7 minutes

 Servings: 4

INGREDIENTS

- 4 salmon fillets, boneless
- 1 tbsp. olive oil
- 1 sliced red onion
- salt
- black pepper
- 1 tsp. ground cumin

DESCRIPTION

STEP 1
Heat up a pan with the oil over medium-high heat, add the onion then cook for 2 minutes.

STEP 2
Add the fish, salt, pepper, and the cumin, cook for 4 minutes on each side, divide between plates and serve.

NUTRITIONAL INFORMATION

Calories 300, Fat 14g, Carbs 5g, Protein 20g

DELICIOUS SALMON

 Cooking Difficulty: 2/10

 Cooking Time: 16 minutes

 Servings: 2

INGREDIENTS

- 2 salmon steak
- 1 tbsp. olive oil
- salt
- pepper
- half a lemon
- salad leaves for serving

DESCRIPTION

STEP 1
Heat up a pan with the oil over medium-high heat.

STEP 2
Add fish, salt, and pepper, cook for 4 minutes on each side, divide onto plates and serve with your favorite salad and lemon.

NUTRITIONAL INFORMATION

362 Calories, 7g Fats, 4.7g Carbs, 5.8 Protein

SEARED SALMON AND WHITE BEANS

 Cooking Difficulty: 3/10

 Cooking Time: 15 minutes

 Servings: 2

INGREDIENTS

- 8 oz. salmon fillet
- 1 medium tomato
- 1 the small bulb of fennel
- 15 oz. white beans
- 3 tsps. olive oil

- ¼ c. dry white wine
- 1½ tsps. dijon mustard
- 1 tsp. fennel seed
- ¼ tsp. pepper

NUTRITIONAL INFORMATION

285 Calories, 13g Fat, 19g Carbs, 15g Protein

STEP 1

Begin by heating a tablespoon of olive oil in a large skillet over medium heat.

STEP 2

Add in the sliced fennel and cook for about 6 minutes or until lightly browned.

STEP 3

When this is done, stir in the white wine, tomato, and beans for about 3 minutes.

STEP 4

After the mixture is done cooking, transfer it into a bowl and stir in the chopped fennel, mustard, and a 1/8 teaspoon of pepper.

STEP 5

Before continuing, rinse and dry the pan you just used.

STEP 6

In a small bowl, combine the fennel seed and a 1/8 teaspoon of pepper, and then sprinkle the mixture on both sides of the salmon.

STEP 7

In the pan, heat up the remaining two teaspoons of olive oil over medium-high heat, and then add the salmon. Cook for 3-6 minutes or until golden brown. Be sure to cook both sides of the salmon.

STEP 8

Last, place the beans onto a plate and top with the salmon. Your meal is complete!

GARLIC SHRIMP

 Cooking Difficulty: 1/10

 Cooking Time: 15 minutes

 Servings: 4

INGREDIENTS

- 2 pounds of peeled shrimp
- salt
- pepper
- 4 cloves garlic
- lemon
- olive oil

DESCRIPTION

STEP 1
Mix garlic, spices and oil together.

STEP 2
Wash shrimp and dip each one in garlic oil.

STEP 3
Drizzle the shrimp with lemon juice and fry for 4 minutes on each side.

STEP 4
Serve hot.

NUTRITIONAL INFORMATION

210 Calories, 7g Fats, 4g Carbs, and 4g Protein

FISH TACOS

 Cooking Difficulty: 2/10	Cooking Time: 10 minutes	Servings: 2

INGREDIENTS

- 1 tbsp. tomato puree
- 1 tbsp. salsa
- 1 tbsp. light mayonnaise
- 2 cod fillets, de-boned, skinless, and cubed
- 1 tbsp. coconut oil
- 1 tbsp. cilantro, chopped
- 4 taco shells, whole wheat
- 1 red onion, chopped

DESCRIPTION

STEP 1
Heat up a pan with the oil over medium heat, add the onion, stir and cook for 2 minutes.

STEP 2
Add the fish and tomato puree, toss gently, and cook for 5 minutes more.

STEP 3
Spoon this into the taco shells, also divide the mayo, salsa, and serve for lunch.

NUTRITIONAL INFORMATION

Calories 306, Fat 14.5g, Carbs 16.6g, Protein 12.9g

SEA BASS

 Cooking Difficulty: 2/10

 Cooking Time: 18 minutes

 Servings: 2

INGREDIENTS

- 2 lemons
- 1/3 c. green olives
- 1 c. grated cauliflower
- 1 seabass
- pepper
- salt
- 1/3 c. chopped parsley
- 1/3 c. chopped mint

DESCRIPTION

STEP 1
Allow the oven to heat up to 400 degrees. Place some parchment paper on a baking pan and place the fish on top. Add some oil to the fish.

STEP 2
Slice the lemons and stuff them into the bass along with the herbs. Place into the oven to bake for 15 minutes.

STEP 3
Chop up the olives and juice the other lemons. Take out a bowl and mix together the rest of the ingredients.

STEP 4
Serve the prepared fish with the cauliflower salad.

NUTRITIONAL INFORMATION

380 Calories, 26g Fats, 3.4g Carbs, 11g Protein

RADISH SALMON SALAD

 Cooking Difficulty: 1/10

 Cooking Time: 3 minutes

 Servings: 2

INGREDIENTS

- 1 grilled and sliced salmon steak
- 2 tablespoons olive oil
- 8 sliced radishes
- 2 tbsp. lemon juice
- black pepper
- salt
- favorite lettuce leaves

DESCRIPTION

STEP 1

In a bowl, mix the radishes slices with the salmon and the rest of the ingredients, stir and serve for lunch.

NUTRITIONAL INFORMATION

Calories 300, Fat 8g, Carbs 5g, Protein 6g

GINGER HALIBUT

 Cooking Difficulty: 2/10

 Cooking Time: 18 minutes

 Servings: 3

INGREDIENTS

- 24 oz. Alaskan halibut fillets
- 1½ tbsps. minced fresh ginger
- 1½ tsps. soy sauce
- 1½ tsps. olive oil
- ¾ tsp. rice wine vinegar

DESCRIPTION

STEP 1
Set the oven to 400 degrees F to preheat. Line a baking sheet with aluminum foil and set it aside.

STEP 2
Combine rice vinegar and olive oils in a bowl, then stir in the soy sauce, and ginger. Add the fish fillets and turn several times to coat.

STEP 3
Arrange the fish fillets on the prepared baking sheet—Bake for 17 minutes, or until done

NUTRITIONAL INFORMATION

380 Calories, 6g Fats, 3.4g Carbs, 7g Protein

POULTRY RECIPES

CHICKEN COUSCOUS

 Cooking Difficulty: 2/10

 Cooking Time: 17 minutes

 Servings: 8

INGREDIENTS

- 3 c. chopped chicken
- 1 ¼ c. chicken broth
- 1 pint grape tomatoes
- 1 tsp. lemon rind
- 1 5.6 oz. package of toasted pine nut couscous mix
- ¼ c. chopped fresh basil
- ¼ tsp. pepper
- salt

DESCRIPTION

STEP 1
You will want to begin this by heating the chicken broth and the seasoning packet from the couscous in a microwave for three to five minutes while on high.

STEP 2
Once the broth is boiling, mix it with the couscous in a large bowl and allow it to stand for about five minutes. Once the time has passed, fluff the couscous with a fork and stir in the chicken.

STEP 4
When this is complete, mix in your spices and vegetables. Your meal is complete!

NUTRITIONAL INFORMATION

334 Calories, 10.9g Fat, 15.8g Carbs, 20.9g Protein

CHICKEN PIECES

 Cooking Difficulty: 3/10	Cooking Time: 15 minutes	Servings: 6

NUTRITIONAL INFORMATION

294 Calories, 5.2g Fat, 12.1g Carbs, 22.2g Protein

INGREDIENTS

- 2 tbsps. lemon juice
- 14 oz. greek yogurt
- 2 tsps. chopped oregano leaves
- ¼ c. white dry wine
- ¼ c. olive oil
- ½ tsp. pepper - divided
- 1 tsp. salt
- 2 lb. skinned breasts
- 4 minced garlic cloves
- 2 tsps. distilled white vinegar
- ½ c. cucumber

DESCRIPTION

STEP 1
Cut the chicken into ½-inch cubes, and coarsely shred the cucumber.

STEP 2
Set the grill between 450°F and 550°F.

STEP 3
Blend the wine, oil, chicken, oregano, lime juice, ¼ teaspoon of pepper, and salt in a mixing bowl.

STEP 4
Use eight metal skewers to prepare the chicken for cooking. Grill for approximately 10-12 minutes.

STEP 5
Remove any excess moisture from the cucumbers with paper towels, and put them into a medium dish. Mix in the yogurt, garlic, vinegar, and pepper with the cucumbers.

STEP 6
Serve with warm pita bread and chicken. Place remaining portions in an airtight container and refrigerate for up to 3 days.

CHICKEN IN TOMATO SAUCE

 Cooking Difficulty: 2/10

 Cooking Time: 27 minutes

 Servings: 3

INGREDIENTS

- 6 chicken drumsticks
- 1 tbsp. cider vinegar
- 1.5 c. tomatillo sauce
- 1 tsp. olive oil
- 1 tsp. dried oregano
- 1/8 tsp. black pepper
- 1 tsp. salt
- ¼ c. chopped cilantro
- 1 jalapeno, halved and seeded

DESCRIPTION

STEP 1
Season the chicken with salt, vinegar, pepper, oregano and marinate them for 2-hours. Set your instant pot to the sauté mode, add the oil, and heat it.

STEP 2
Saute the chicken until the meat is browned. After frying the chicken, add all the other ingredients (except for the cilantro) and shut the lid to the pot. Set on Manual mode on high, with a cook time of 20-minutes.

STEP 3
When the cooking time is completed, release the pressure using quick-release. Garnish with chopped cilantro just before serving.

NUTRITIONAL INFORMATION

Calories: 302, Fat: 13g, Carbs: 10g, Protein: 32g

TERIYAKI CHICKEN

 Cooking Difficulty: 2/10	Cooking Time: 20 minutes	Servings: 2

INGREDIENTS

- 1 chicken filet
- 2 spoons of teriyaki sauce
- 1 spoonful of soy sauce
- green onions for decoration

DESCRIPTION

STEP 1
Cut the chicken fillet into small slices.

STEP 2
Heat a frying pan. Add the chicken to the pan and stir-fry. When the chicken is almost done, add the two sauces. Sauté the chicken so all the moisture is gone and the glaze comes out.

STEP 3
Serve with green onions and rice.

NUTRITIONAL INFORMATION

411 Calories, 11g Fats, 6g Carbs, 4.8 Protein

TURKEY MEATBALLS WITH TOMATO SAUCE

Cooking Difficulty: 3/10	Cooking Time: 25 minutes	Servings: 4

NUTRITIONAL INFORMATION

380 Calories, 16g Fats, 5g Carbs, 8g Protein

INGREDIENTS

- 7 oz. chopped fresh mushrooms
- 1 chopped onion
- 1 lightly beaten egg
- 1 tbsp. italian seasoning
- 14.5 oz. diced tomatoes
- 2 lb. lean ground turkey
- 2 tbsps. olive oil

DESCRIPTION

STEP 1

In a medium-size bowl, combine mushrooms, egg, ground turkey, onion and Italian seasoning. Shape the mixture into meatballs.

STEP 2

Heat a nonstick skillet over medium heat. Add oil. Cook meatballs until brown, and there is no pink in the center or for four minutes with frequent stirring.

STEP 3

Remove from the pan and keep warm. Add tomatoes into the pan, let it boil, and simmer for 15 mins. or until thickens.

STEP 4

Add the cooked meatballs into the pan with tomatoes and simmer for around 5 minutes or until heated through.

CABBAGE AND CHICKEN MIX

 Cooking Difficulty: 3/10

 Cooking Time: 22 minutes

 Servings: 4

INGREDIENTS

- ¼ tsp. red pepper, crushed
- ¼ c. chicken stock
- ¾ c. red bell peppers, chopped
- 3 tomatoes, cubed
- ¼ c. green onions, chopped
- 1 yellow onion, chopped
- 1 lb. chicken ground
- 1 green cabbage head, shredded
- 1 tbsp. olive oil
- salt
- pepper

DESCRIPTION

STEP 1
Heat up a pan with the oil over medium heat, add the chicken and the onions, stir and brown for 5 minutes.

STEP 2
Add the cabbage and the other ingredients, toss, cook for 15 minutes, divide into bowls and serve for lunch.

STEP 2
Place remaining portions in an airtight container and refrigerate for up to 3 days.

NUTRITIONAL INFORMATION

340 Calories, 10g Fats, 4g Carbs, 4.9 Protein

BAKED CHICKEN WITH SWEET PAPRIKA

Cooking Difficulty: 2/10	Cooking Time: 35 minutes	Servings: 4

INGREDIENTS

- 4 chicken fillets
- 2 tbsp. sweet paprika
- 3 tbsp. olive oil
- 3 tbsp. dried garlic
- salt
- black pepper

DESCRIPTION

STEP 1
Preheat oven to 380 F.

STEP 2
Rub the chicken fillet with spices and olive oil and let sit for 5 minutes.

STEP 3
Place the chicken in the oven and bake for 30 minutes.

STEP 4
Serve with salad or chopped vegetables.

NUTRITIONAL INFORMATION

Calories 298, Fat 9,3g, Carbs 6g, Protein 11g

CHICKEN AND VEGGIES TORTILLA SOUP

 Cooking Difficulty: 4/10	Cooking Time: 132 minutes	Servings: 8

NUTRITIONAL INFORMATION

230 Calories, 8.3g Carbs, 31.6g Protein, 7.5g Fat

INGREDIENTS

- 28 oz. diced tomatoes
- 1 bunch chopped cilantro
- 1 diced sweet onion
- 1 tsp. chili powder
- 2 c. water
- 2 c. chopped celery
- 2 c. shredded carrots
- 2 chicken breasts
- 2 tbsps. tomato paste
- 32 oz. chicken broth
- 4 cloves minced garlic
- olive oil
- salt
- pepper

DESCRIPTION

STEP 1
Heat a large Dutch oven or crockpot over medium-high heat, add a dash of olive oil and ¼ c. of chicken broth.

STEP 2
Add garlic, salt, pepper and onion and cook until soft, adding broth as needed.

STEP 3
Add all the remaining ingredients and water to fill the pot. Cover and cook for 2 hours on low and add pepper and salt to taste if needed.

STEP 4
Shred the cooked chicken using the back of a wooden spoon and pressing it at the side of the pot. You can also use tongs or fork to break the chicken apart and shreds it.

STEP 5
Top with fresh cilantro and avocado slices. Serve.

SNACKS & DESSERTS

161

AVOCADO SLICES

 Cooking Difficulty: 1/10	Cooking Time: 4 minutes	Servings: 2

NUTRITIONAL INFORMATION

160 Calories, 9g Fats, 2g Carbs, 1g Protein

INGREDIENTS

- 2 ripe avocados
- ¼ c. coconut cream, whipped
- 1 c. almond meal
- 1 c. olive oil
- 1 cayenne pepper
- salt
  chili dip:
- 1 c. extra-virgin olive oil
- ½ c. almond milk
- 2 tsps. cider vinegar
- 1 tsp. chili powder
- salt

DESCRIPTION

STEP 1
Peel, pit, and slice avocados.

STEP 2
Place whipped coconut cream in a small bowl.

STEP 3
In a separate bowl, combine almond meal with salt and cayenne pepper.

STEP 4
Heat oil in a deep pan.

STEP 5
Place avocado pieces into the heated oil and fry 45 seconds.

STEP 6
Transfer to a paper-lined plate.

STEP 7
Make a chili dip; blend all dip ingredients, except the oil, in a food blender until smooth. Stream in oil and blend until creamy. Serve with avocado slices.

FRIED MUSHROOMS

 Cooking Difficulty: 2/10

 Cooking Time: 23 minutes

 Servings: 3

INGREDIENTS

- 1 lb mushrooms, halved
- 1 large onion
- 2 cloves garlic minced
- salt and pepper to taste
- 2 tablespoons of olive oil
- 1 tablespoon Worcestershire Sauce (optional)
- parsley
- italian herbs (optional)

DESCRIPTION

STEP 1
Heat a frying pan and add olive oil to it. Pour in the Worcestershire sauce.

STEP 2
Add the mushrooms and cook until golden brown, about 5 minutes. Add the onions and cook until the edges are browned and the onions are translucent. Stir in the mushrooms as they roast.

STEP 3
At the last minute, reduce the heat to low and add the crushed garlic, stirring continuously. Salt and pepper to taste. Garnish with parsley and serve.

NUTRITIONAL INFORMATION

111 Calories, 6g Fats, 3g Carbs, 6.8 Protein

KALE AND ALMONDS

 Cooking Difficulty: 2/10

 Cooking Time: 8 minutes

 Servings: 4

INGREDIENTS

- 1 c. water
- 1 big kale bunch, chopped
- 1 tbsp. balsamic vinegar
- 1/3 c. toasted almonds
- 3 minced garlic cloves
- 1 small chopped yellow onion
- 2 tbsps. olive oil

DESCRIPTION

STEP 1
Set your instant pot on sauté mode, add oil, heat it up, add onion, stir and cook for 3 minutes.

STEP 2
Add garlic, water and kale, stir, cover and cook on High for 4 minutes.

STEP 3
Add salt, pepper, vinegar, and almonds, toss well, divide between plates and serve as a side dish.

STEP 4
Enjoy!

NUTRITIONAL INFORMATION

140 Calories, 6g Fat, 1g Carbs, 3g Protein

167

ZUCCHINI DIP

 Cooking Difficulty: 2/10	Cooking Time: 12 minutes	Servings: 4

INGREDIENTS

- 2 spring onions, chopped
- ¼ c. veggie stock
- 2 garlic cloves, minced
- 2 zucchinis, chopped
- 1 tbsp. olive oil
- ½ c. yogurt
- 1 tbsp. dill, chopped

DESCRIPTION

STEP 1
Heat up a pan with the oil over medium heat, add the onions and garlic, stir and sauté for 3 minutes.

STEP 2
Add the zucchinis and the other ingredients except the yogurt, toss, cook for 7 minutes more and take off the heat.

STEP 3
Add the yogurt, blend using an immersion blender, divide into bowls, and serve.

NUTRITIONAL INFORMATION

Calories 76, Fat 4.1, Carbs 7.2, Protein 3.4

DELICIOUS HUMMUS

 Cooking Difficulty: 1/10

 Cooking Time: 4 minutes

 Servings: 6

INGREDIENTS

- ¾ dried chickpeas
- 2 tbsps. olive oil
- 2/3 c. tahini paste
- juice of 2 lemons
- salt
- black pepper
- extra virgin olive oil for

  sprinkling

DESCRIPTION

STEP 1
Put the chickpeas in a large bowl with cold water and allow it to soak.

STEP 2
Drain and put in a saucepan with enough water to cover. Bring to a boil. Simmer on reduced heat for 1 hour, until chickpeas are soft and tender.

STEP 3
Transfer the chick-peas to a food processor and blend well to see a puree. Add in the olive oil, lemon juice, tahini paste. Mix well until smooth and consistent. Season with pepper and salt.

NUTRITIONAL INFORMATION

408 Calories, 23.6g Fats, 25.2g Net Carbs, 19.4g Protein

CAULIFLOWER POPCORN

 Cooking Difficulty: 1/10

 Cooking Time: 480 minutes

 Servings: 4

INGREDIENTS

- 2 tbsps. olive oil
- 2 tsps. chili powder
- 1 tbsp. nutritional yeast
- 1 head cauliflower
- salt

DESCRIPTION

STEP 1
Before you begin making this recipe, you will want to take a few moments to cut your cauliflower into bite-sized pieces, like popcorn.

STEP 2
Once your cauliflower is set, place it into a mixing bowl and coat with the olive oil. Once coated properly, add in the nutritional yeast, salt, and the rest of the spices.

STEP 3
You can enjoy your snack immediately or place into a dehydrator at 115 for 8 hours. By doing this, it will make the cauliflower crispy! You can really enjoy it either way.

NUTRITIONAL INFORMATION
Calories: 100, Carbs: 10g, Fats: 5g, Proteins: 5g

CHOCOLATE MOUSSE

 Cooking Difficulty: 1/10

 Cooking Time: 15 minutes

 Servings: 5

INGREDIENTS

- 170 g dairy-free dark chocolate
- 2 tablespoons cocoa powder
- 1 teaspoon vanilla bean paste
- 3 tablespoons maple syrup
- 1 x 160 g tin of coconut cream

DESCRIPTION

STEP 1

Place a heatproof bowl over a pot of boiling water, making sure that the bottom does not touch the water. You should have a kind of steam bath. Break the chocolate into the bowl and let it melt, then set it aside to cool slightly.

STEP 2

Pestle the remaining ingredients into the brander and mix for a few seconds. Pour in the cooled chocolate and whisk again until creamy.

STEP 3

Divide the mixture into 5 small bowls and chill in the fridge for at least 30 minutes. Serve.

NUTRITIONAL INFORMATION

280 Calories, 11g Fats, 6g Carbs, and 3,8g Protein

VEGAN PANNA COTTA

 Cooking Difficulty: 2/10

 Cooking Time: 20 minutes

 Servings: 2

INGREDIENTS

- 1 14-ounce can of full-fat coconut milk
- 1 tablespoon of maple syrup
- 1 teaspoon of vanilla extract
- 1 1/2 teaspoons of agar agar powder
- 1/2 cup of water
- 1/2 cup of fresh or frozen strawberries
- 2 tablespoons of maple syrup
- 1 tablespoon of lemon juice

NUTRITIONAL INFORMATION

Calories: 239, Fats: 21g, Carbs: 12g, Protein: 2g

STEP 1

In a saucepan, whisk together the coconut milk, maple syrup, and vanilla extract. Heat the mixture over medium heat until well combined.

STEP 2

In a separate bowl, whisk together the agar agar powder and water. Add the agar agar mixture to the coconut milk mixture and whisk until well combined.

STEP 3

Bring the mixture to a simmer over medium heat, stirring constantly. Cook for 2-3 minutes, or until the agar agar has dissolved and the mixture has thickened.

STEP 4

Pour the mixture into two small ramekins or glasses. Let cool to room temperature, then refrigerate for at least 2 hours, or until set.

STEP 5

While the panna cotta is setting, make the strawberry jam. In a small saucepan, combine the strawberries, maple syrup, and lemon juice. Cook over medium heat, stirring occasionally, until the strawberries have broken down and the mixture has thickened, about 10-12 minutes.

STEP 6

Once the panna cotta is set, top each with a spoonful of strawberry jam.

STEP 7

Serve immediately, garnished with additional strawberries if desired.

ORANGE SMOOTHIE

 **Cooking Difficulty:** 1/10

 Cooking Time: 2 minutes

 Servings: 1

INGREDIENTS

- 6 ice cubes
- ¾ c. coconut milk
- 1 scoop vanilla whey protein
- 2 tbsps. coconut oil
- 2 oz. plain skyr
- 8 oz. fresh orange juice
- 2 oz. shredded carrot
- 1 ripe mango

DESCRIPTION

STEP 1
Cream the coconut milk: This is a simple process. All you need to do is place the can of coconut milk in the refrigerator overnight. The next morning, open the can and spoon out the coconut milk that has solidified. Don't shake the can before opening. Discard the liquids.

STEP 2
Add all of the ingredients, save the ice cubes, to the blender, and blend on low speed until pureed. Thin with water as needed. Add in the ice cubes and blend until the smoothie reaches your desired consistency.

NUTRITIONAL INFORMATION

328 Calories, 7g Carbs, 7g Fats, 8g Protein

MARINATED OLIVES

 Cooking Difficulty: 1/10

 Cooking Time: 2 minutes

 Servings: 8

INGREDIENTS

- 1 1/3 c. green olives
- 4 tbsps. chopped coriander
- 1 crushed garlic clove
- 1 tsp. grated ginger
- 1 sliced red chili
- ¼ lemon

DESCRIPTION

STEP 1
Press the olives to break slightly, soak in cold water overnight, and then drain.

STEP 2
Mix well the ingredients and pour into the jars to marinade the olives. Place the jar in the fridge for at least 1 week, shaking 2-3 time.

NUTRITIONAL INFORMATION

404.7 Calories, 40.0g Fats, 13.1g Carbs, 0.5g Protein

CONCLUSION

Thanks for reading this book. I hope this guide on the Flexitarian diet has provided you with enough insight to get you going. Don't put off getting started. The sooner you begin this diet, the sooner you'll start to notice an improvement in your health and well-being. Start to care about the health of your heart immediately. While results won't come overnight, they will come if you stick to the information provided throughout this book.

Furthermore, it is my hope that you enjoy all the healthy recipes in this book. There's no shortage of meals you can enjoy on a Flexitarian diet. Having said that, the next step is to experiment with the different recipes. Enjoy the journey!

Jerry Carr

Made in the USA
Monee, IL
12 May 2023

33544621R00103